RV Living Cookbook
Real Recipes for the RV Lifestyle

By Tracy Perkins
www.camperchronicles.com

Thank you to all of my friends and family who shared their recipes with me for this book. I am very grateful for your generosity and support.

This book is dedicated to my husband Lee. Not only for his willingness to be my taste tester, but for his unflagging support and encouragement throughout the two years it took to develop these recipes.

It never would have happened without you honey.

Copyright © 2017 by Tracy S. Perkins
All rights reserved. This book or any portion thereof may not be reproduced or used in any manner whatsoever without the express written permission of the author.

www.camperchronicles.com

Introduction

Magma Pans

Weber Grill

Presto Fryer

Cooking in an RV can be a very different experience from cooking in a home, and for those who live all or part of the year in an RV, it can be quite challenging. Limited ingredients, different appliances and lack of space for food prep will often have an impact on what food people cook.

I learned that lesson pretty early, because despite twenty five years of experience cooking for my family I struggled with cooking in our RV. So I started gathering recipes that I felt actually worked. I also rediscovered my joy of cooking, and working with new ingredients as we visited different areas of the country became a wonderful challenge.

As we have traveled I have gathered recipes from fellow RVers, local resources, and modified some family favorites to work in our RV. Only a small portion of the recipes I tried actually made this book, and the recipes I am sharing here were our absolute favorites. They are all real recipe prepared and eaten by us in our RV.

Most are pretty simple. For me, the perfect recipe has ingredients and prep time proportional to taste. I'm happy to do more work if the taste is amazing, but my preference will always be a small amount of common ingredients with relatively simple preparation which leads to amazing taste.

There are some exceptions, of course. I have listed the recipes within each section from simplest to most complicated, and in each section there are a few that were definitely worth the extra trouble. The recipes are also grouped by RV specific categories, to make it simpler to look for something to make depending on the situation.

Thank you for purchasing this book. I hope you find the recipes as delicious as we do and they add some fun to your own adventures.

Tracy Perkins
www.camperchronicles.com

Table of Contents

Collapsible Bowls

Instant Pot

Wok

Happy Hour

Pot Luck Dishes

Travel Days

Pressure Cooker

Dinners For Two

Side Dishes

Regional Specialties

Desserts

Happy Hour

One thing RVers do well is celebrate happy hour. It's common for them to gather for appetizers and drinks when they get together in any number, from a few couples to a full blown rally. These gatherings are often impromptu affairs, but people usually bring something to snack on. Quick and easy recipes that can be made with food on hand is often called for, although sometimes more elaborate menu items are made outside, which adds to the fun. After all, we don't want to miss the party!

Kelly's Queso Dip

This recipe is one of Lee's favorites and is easy to make. The ingredients can easily be stored for long periods of time, so it's perfect for impromptu gatherings.

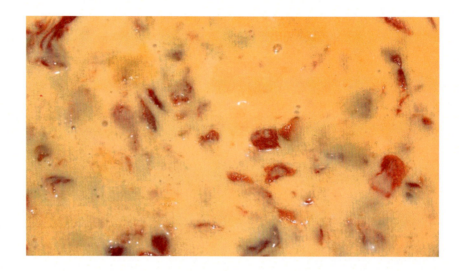

SERVES [8]

INGREDIENTS

1 lb Velveeta® cheese
Kelly recommends Queso Blanco

1 small can Rotel® tomatoes

DIRECTIONS

1. Cut up cheese and microwave slowly (50% power) until partially melted.
2. Drain can of Rotel® very well and then add to cheese.
3. Mix well.
4. Microwave to desired consistency (again using 50% power).
5. Serve with tortilla chips or crackers.

Dill Dip

I love vegetables and dip, but I am pretty picky about my dip. This recipe is my favorite and contains ingredients people usually have on-hand.

SERVES [8]

INGREDIENTS

1 cup mayonnaise
1 cup sour cream
1 tbsp dill weed
1/4 tsp seasoning salt
1 TBL dried onion flakes (or substitute fresh green onions)

DIRECTIONS

1. In a medium bowl mix together all ingredients.
2. Chill the ingredients for at least 30 minutes.
3. Stir dip.
4. Serve with raw vegetables, preferably those found in a local farmers market.

Carol's Bread and Olive Oil Dip

Bread and dipping sauce is the perfect complement to a glass of wine with friends and it's easy on the budget. You can use many different types of bread, but my favorite is thinly sliced Italian bread.

SERVES [6]

INGREDIENTS

1 cup high quality extra virgin light olive oil
2 small cloves of garlic; minced or crushed
1 tsp garlic powder
1 tsp Italian herb seasoning or oregano
Pinch of salt
Pinch of pepper
5-6 red pepper flakes (more to taste)
 Italian or French bread

DIRECTIONS

1. Add dry ingredients in bowl and mix well.
2. Add crushed or minced garlic.
3. Add 1 cup of extra virgin olive oil.
4. Stir well then let sit for at least 15 minutes.
5. Stir prior to serving.
6. Serve with warm, sliced bread.

Pam's Chili Cheese Dip

This recipe is another great one for impromptu gatherings. Pam keeps the ingredients on hand so she can throw it together any time.

SERVES [8]

INGREDIENTS

8 oz cream cheese
1 can of chili (with or without beans)
2 cups shredded cheese (Mexican blend or cheddar)

DIRECTIONS

1. Spread cream cheese in 8x8 pan.
2. Spread chili on top.
3. Spread shredded cheese.
4. Bake at 400° for 30 minutes.
5. Serve either stirred or in layers with chips.

Stromboli

I'm not a huge fan of Stromboli, but this recipe I like because the pizza sauce is served on the side. Plus it's pretty easy to make and great to feed a crowd.

SERVES [6]

INGREDIENTS

10 oz loaf of frozen bread; dough, thawed
1/4 lb thin sliced ham
1/4 lb thin sliced pepperoni
3 oz sliced provolone cheese
1 cup (4 oz) shredded mozzarella cheese
1 TBL melted butter
Pizza Sauce; served on the side as a dipping sauce

DIRECTIONS

1. Allow bread to thaw and rise per instructions.
2. Place dough on lightly greased baking sheet.
3. Pat to a 15" x 10" rectangle.
4. Arrange mozzarella cheese lengthwise down the center.
5. Place pepperoni on dough then provolone cheese, then ham.
6. Moisten edges of dough with water.
7. Bring each end of dough to center and press edges together; use more water if needed.
8. Brush loaf with melted butter mixed with a little pizza sauce if desired.
9. Bake at 375° for 20 minutes or until lightly browned.
10. Cool a little, then cut into slices with a bread knife.
11. Serve warm with pizza sauce for dipping.

Lee's Favorite Deviled Eggs

Who doesn't love deviled eggs? That's why even though they are time consuming to make I keep making them. This recipe has been with us since we first got married and Lee still gets that "this is yummy" look in his eyes when he eats one of these eggs

SERVES [12]

INGREDIENTS

2 dozen eggs
1/4 tsp onion salt
1/4 tsp celery salt
1/4 tsp garlic salt
1 cup mayonnaise
6 squirts yellow mustard
paprika
sliced green olives

DIRECTIONS

1. Hard boil eggs.
2. Run cold water over eggs, then place in refrigerator until chilled.
3. Peel eggs.
4. Slice eggs in half longways.
5. Remove yolks and place in bowl.
6. Using a fork break yolks into very small pieces.
7. Add mayonnaise, mustard, garlic, celery, and onion salt.
8. Mix very well with a fork.
9. Using a small spoon place egg mixture into the center of the egg whites.
10. Sprinkle with paprika (if desired).
11. Cut olives and place a slice (without pimento) on each egg (if desired).

Bill's Amazing Chicken Wings

These wings taste just like what you would get in a restaurant. They definitely take some time to cook, but they're totally worth the effort. Plus you can fry them outside and still be part of the party!

SERVES [12]

INGREDIENTS

Frank's Hot Sauce®
<u>Fresh</u> chicken wings
Butter or margarine
Oil
Ranch Dressing
Blue Cheese Dressing
Celery Sticks

DIRECTIONS

1. Cut chicken portions into drums and wings.
2. Boil in hot oil (completely submerged) for 8-12 minutes.
3. Carefully remove from oil and let drain on paper towels.
4. Prepare coating; equal parts hot sauce and butter.
5. Toss wings with coating until well covered.
6. Serve with blue cheese and/or ranch dressing.
7. Garnish with celery sticks

Crawfish or Shrimp Beignets

You probably won't have the raw ingredients on hand to make these and they are also are not quick and easy to make, but wow they are good. And once again, you can fry these while standing outside and having a nice beverage.

SERVES [4]

INGREDIENTS

1 lb Crawfish or shrimp meat
1 egg
4 green onions
1-1/2 tsp butter; melted
1/2 tsp salt
1/2 tsp cayenne pepper
1/3 cup flour

Dipping Sauce
3/4 cup mayonnaise
1/4 tsp prepared horseradish
1/4 tsp pepper sauce

DIRECTIONS

1. In a large bowl combine meat, egg, onions, butter, salt, and cayenne pepper.
2. Stir in flour until blended.
3. Heat oil to 375° in wok, deep skillet, or fryer.
4. Drop tablespoons of mixture into oil; a few at a time.
5. Fry until golden brown on both sides.
6. Drain on paper towels.
7. Serve with Louisiana dipping sauce or make your own.

Dipping Sauce
1. Combine dipping sauce ingredients.
2. Stir well.
3. Allow to sit at least 15 minutes before serving.

Sue's Black Bean Rally Dip

Sue's dip has multiple ingredients and takes some time to make. On the plus side it reheats well and can be prepared in advance. Oh and did I mention Lee is in love with this dip? It's a good thing she taught me how to make it.

SERVES [10] UNLESS LEE IS EATING IT THEN MAYBE 4

INGREDIENTS

1 lb hamburger
4 Hot Johnson Sausages
1 medium yellow onion; chopped
2 cans black beans (15 oz) (drained slightly)
1 red pepper
1 yellow pepper
1 bag of frozen corn (16 oz)
2 pkg taco seasoning (no water)
1 can jalapeño chilies (4 oz)
1 can fire roasted tomatoes (15 oz)
1 tsp garlic powder
1 tsp black pepper
1 tsp cumin
1 tsp cilantro
1 cup shredded Jack and Cheddar cheese blend

DIRECTIONS

1. Blend hamburger and finely chopped Hot Johnson sausages and brown over medium heat.
2. Mix all other ingredients (except cheese) in a large bowl.
3. Mix in cooked hamburger/sausage mixture.
4. Portion out any parts you would like to freeze.
5. Place remaining in a covered glass casserole dish and microwave for 20 minutes (reduce microwave time to 10 minutes if you are heating a smaller batch.
6. Remove dish and sprinkle with cheese.
7. Microwave for 1 more minute or until cheese is melted Serve with tortilla chips *Lee likes the scoops so he can get more dip per bite!*

Vietnamese Fried Egg Rolls with Fish Oil Dipping Sauce

To be completely honest this recipe is a crazy amount of work. But Vietnamese egg rolls are my absolute favorite appetizer. I went on a quest to find a way to make this in the RV and here is the result. You may not find the results worth the effort, but I absolutely do!

SERVES [4]

INGREDIENTS

Spring Roll Wrappers
2 tbsp peanut oil
2 cloves garlic; crushed
1/2 lb lean pork; ground or diced
4 scallions; thinly chopped
1/4 cup grated radish
2 tbsp fish sauce
2 oz cellophane noodles; soaked in warm water for 15 minutes
You can substitute bean sprouts for noodles
Peanut oil for frying

Dipping Sauce
1 cup boiling water
1/2 cup sugar
1/4 cup fish sauce
3 tbsp White Vinegar
Red pepper flakes; optional

DIRECTIONS

1. Heat wok and add oil and garlic. Stir for a moment then add pork.
2. Stir for a couple of minutes then add all remaining ingredients.
3. Stir for a couple more minutes until all ingredients are hot.
4. Allow mixture to cool.
5. Place water in a small bowl.
6. Place one spring roll wrapper in front of you in diamond shape.
7. Brush edges of wrapper with water.
8. Place a tablespoon of mixture near the top point of diamond then roll once towards you.
9. Tuck in sides and complete roll.
10. Place on baking sheet; seam side down.
11. Repeat with remaining filling and wrappers.
12. Heat fryer with peanut oil to 375°.
13. Cook in small batches until golden brown.
14. Serve with fish oil dipping sauce and/or sweet and sour dipping sauce

Dipping Sauce
1. Boil water then take off burner
2. Add sugar and stir until it dissolves
3. Add white vinegar one tbsp at a time until you like the taste.
4. Add grated carrots, grated radish, or red pepper flakes
5. Allow to sit for at least 1 hour before serving

Potluck Dishes

....

One of my husband's favorite parts of RVing is sharing meals with our friends. Their "old standard" recipes are all new to us, and you never know when you will find an amazing new recipe. Despite the "luck" in the title. we like to organize these dinners with some level of coordination.

If it is a small group we want to make sure that all of the major components are covered (ie: meat, vegetables, salad, desert) and if we are all eating together frequently we want to make sure that the higher cost main dishes are spread evenly amongst the group over time. With a big group it's also a great idea to provide food label cards so diners with food allergies/restrictions know what is safe for them to eat.

Barb's Cucumber Salad

This is Lee's absolute favorite salad. It is flavorful, easy to make, and holds up well in the refrigerator. I've been making it for him since we were newly married

SERVES [4]

INGREDIENTS

1 large cucumber
1/3 large red onion
1 cup mayonnaise
1/3 cup of cider vinegar
Pepper

DIRECTIONS

1. Cut off ends of cucumbers and then use a peeler to cut away three thin strips lengthwise as shown in picture.
2. Cut cucumber horizontally into thin slices.
3. Cut onion into small squares about 1".
4. Mix onions and cucumbers in a plastic bowl with a lid.
5. Add mayonnaise to vegetables.
6. Add cider vinegar to vegetables.
7. Sprinkle with pepper.
8. Place lid on bowl and shake or mix with slotted spoon.
9. Sprinkle with pepper and mix again.
10. It's best after being chilled overnight.

Broccoli and Cheese Casserole

This was my mom's go-to pot luck dish and I have always loved this recipe. Real butter is a key ingredient and you can easily double this recipe for a larger group.

SERVES [6]

INGREDIENTS

1/2 Velveeta® cheese
1 tube Ritz® Crackers

1 stick real butter

16 oz bag frozen broccoli

DIRECTIONS

1. Cook and drain broccoli. Press between a clean dishcloth to get all the moisture out so it is *very* dry.
2. Place broccoli, while still warm, in a saucepan and add cheese cut into small pieces.
3. Stir until cheese is melted, using low heat on stove.
4. Spread cheese and broccoli mixture on bottom of casserole dish; 8x8 for single recipe or 13 x 9 for double recipe.
5. In a small sauce pan melt 1 stick of real butter; remove from heat.
6. Crush crackers (while still in tube); very fine.
7. Add cracker crumbs to butter and mix well.
8. Spread cracker topping evenly on broccoli and cheese.
9. Bake for 20 minutes at 350°.
10. Allow to cool and serve warm.

Mama Gregg's Baked Beans

My grandmother made the absolute best baked beans and when I got married and asked her for the recipe she said she learned to make them from Mrs. Gregg. They can be served warm, but my favorite is eating them the next day cold.

SERVES [12]

INGREDIENTS

Four 16 oz cans of regular pork and beans
1-1/2 cups of brown sugar; firmly packed
2 tbsp Mustard
1 cup ketchup
8-10 slices of bacon
Onion salt; lightly sprinkled

DIRECTIONS

1. Place beans in a large pot.
2. Add brown sugar, mustard, and ketchup and mix.
3. In a large pan cook bacon until limp; cut into quarters.
4. Pour bacon and grease into bean pot and stir well.
5. Sprinkle lightly with onion salt.
6. Heat beans slowly to boiling; then reduce to simmer.
6. Simmer for 1-2 hours stirring occasionally.
7. Serve warm.
8. Refrigerate leftovers.
9. Eat cold the next day. So good!

Crunchy Cole Slaw

This is my go-to pot luck item. It is easy to make, relatively inexpensive,and goes with anything. This recipe does have peanuts though and just doesn't taste the same without them. If you are serving it at a big potluck, make sure and mark the dish.

SERVES [8]

INGREDIENTS

One 16 oz package of coleslaw mix
1 large carrot peeled into thin strips
1/2 medium-sized red onion (chopped)
1 cup cocktail peanuts (shelled and split)
1/2 cup canola oil
1/3 cup cider vinegar
1-1/2 tsp sugar
1/2 tsp celery salt

DIRECTIONS

1. In a large bowl combine vegetables and mix well.
2. In a small bowl whisk remaining ingredients.
3. Pour dressing over salad and toss well to coat.

Sugar Free French Toast Casserole

Some pot lucks are breakfasts or brunch and this sugar free French toast is a great choice. Just remember to start it the night before.

SERVES [10]

INGREDIENTS

5 cups of cubed bread
4 eggs
1-1/2 cups of milk
1 tsp vanilla extract
Cinnamon
1/4 cup Splenda®
Pam Cooking Spray®

DIRECTIONS

1. Spray baking dish with Pam®.
2. Beat eggs, milk, 2 tablespoons sweetener, 1 teaspoon cinnamon, and vanilla extract together in a bowl.
3. Mix bread with egg/milk mixture above.
4. Pour into pan.
5. Place in refrigerator overnight.
6. Preheat oven to 350°.
7. Sprinkle additional Splenda® and cinnamon mix on top of the casserole.
8. Bake for 30-40 minutes until top is slightly crunchy.

Quickie Donuts

Every once in a while I try a new recipe and it is so simple and delicious that I can't believe I never made it before. This was one of those.

SERVES [6]

INGREDIENTS

1 can refrigerated biscuits
Powdered sugar
Cinnamon; optional

DIRECTIONS

1. Heat oil in fryer or pan to 375°.
2. Use your fingers to make a hole in the center of the biscuit, pushing dough slightly out to form a donut ring.
3. Gently drop biscuit in oil.
4. Cook until golden brown then flip and repeat. Less than one minute per side.
5. Drain.
6. Place in Ziploc® bag with powdered sugar and/or cinnamon while still warm and shake gently until lightly covered.
7. Serve and eat warm.

Quick Pickle Ribbons

Cucumbers are readily available in farmer's markets during the summer and although I am not a huge fan I do love pickles. This recipe turns fresh cucumbers into a yummy pickle-flavored side dish

SERVES [6]

INGREDIENTS

4 medium-sized cucumbers; scrubbed but skin on
2 large carrots; peeled
1/2 small onion; thinly sliced
2 TBL dill weed
1/2 tsp ground black pepper
3/4 cup white vinegar
1/2 cup sugar
1 TBL kosher or sea salt

DIRECTIONS

1. Using a vegetable peeler peel the cucumber lengthwise into long thin ribbons. Stop when you reach the seeds and discard remainder.
2. Using same technique turn peeled carrot into long thin strips stopping when you reach core of carrot and discard remainder.
3. In a large bowl combine cucumber, carrot, onion, dill weed, and pepper.
4. In a small saucepan bring vinegar, sugar, and salt just to boiling over medium-high heat.
5. Pour mixture immediately over vegetables; stir to combine.
6. Cover and chill for 1 hour
7. Serve.

Mom's Cheese Potatoes

One of my favorite dishes is cheese potatoes. They always remind me of the holidays. But because they are somewhat labor intensive, I have put them in the pot luck section. If you are going to make them you might as well share them with friends.

SERVES [12]

INGREDIENTS

6-8 large potatoes
I slice American cheese per potato
1 can evaporated milk
1 stick butter
Paprika

DIRECTIONS

1. Cook potatoes in oven at 400° for one hour.
2. Slice potatoes in half longways.
3. Scoop insides of potatoes out (leaving some to keep skin intact) and place in bowl.
4. Add 1 slice of cheese per potato, 1/2 stick butter. 1/2 cup milk then blend .
5. Add additional milk and/or butter until mixture is somewhat smooth and has the consistency of mashed potatoes.
6. Scoop potato mixture back into potato shells .
7. Sprinkle with paprika.
8. Heat in 350° for 20 minutes until warm then serve.

Connie's Best Ever Potato Salad

Everyone has their favorite potato salad, but mine is hands down my mom's. It takes a while to make and is better the next day, but is so worth it.

SERVES [12]

INGREDIENTS

6-8 medium sized Idaho potatoes
4 hard boiled eggs; yolks and whites separated
3 chopped green onions; thinly sliced including greens
2 cups mayonnaise
2 TBL Plochman's® mild yellow mustard
1 pkg Good Seasons® Italian Dressing

DIRECTIONS

1. Peel potatoes and cut into small pieces.
2. Boil covered until you can easily cut through with a butter knife. Remove before mushy.
3. Rinse with cool water.
4. Hard boil eggs.
5. Allow both eggs and potatoes to cool.
6. Use a fork to mix egg yolks, mayo, mustard, and Good Seasons®.
7. Cut potatoes into bite sized pieces and chop egg whites.
8. Gently mix potatoes, green onions, and egg whites.
9. Gently mix dressing into potato mixture.
10. Refrigerate until served. Best if made the night before.

Watermelon Fruit Basket

Healthy and beautiful, this fruit basket is a great choice for a potluck. Cutting the watermelon is the hardest part.

SERVES [12]

INGREDIENTS

Watermelon
(Oblong shaped)
Grapes; green
and purple
Strawberries
Pineapple

DIRECTIONS

1. Cut top of watermelon, then scallop the edges as shown in picture.
2. Scoop/cut watermelon out and place into a bowl.
3. Rinse inside of watermelon shell; removing seeds.
4. Cut watermelon into bite size pieces.
5. Slice strawberries.
6. Place cut watermelon in the middle of rind.
7. Place a row of strawberries on each side.
8. Place a row of grapes on each end.
9. Put pineapple chunks on top and bottom edges.
10. Mix leftover fruit into a bowl and use to replenish rind when empty or serve separately.

Travel Days

....

Cooking on travel days can be very stressful, but it is also more economical than eating out. We usually want a hot meal at the end of the day, but rarely have the energy for cooking anything complicated, so these recipe have become our travel day go-to's. Some of them are made ahead and frozen, but others can be thrown together when you stop for the day.

Tracy's Chili

Our favorite travel day staple is chili. I make this in large batches and freeze it for travel days. I like it with saltines and butter and Lee likes it with cornbread. Either way it's a great hot meal on a long travel day.

SERVES [10]

INGREDIENTS

3 packages of chili seasoning
3 lbs hamburger
One 15 oz can dark red kidney beans; drained
Two 15 oz cans light red kidney beans; drained
Three 14 oz cans petite diced tomatoes; include juice

DIRECTIONS

1. Brown hamburger and drain.
2. Add tomatoes, kidney beans, and seasoning packets to large pot.
3. Add hamburger and stir.
4. Cook over medium heat until comes to a light boil.
5. Simmer; stirring occasionally so it does not burn.
6. After cool freeze in two portion bags.
7. Thaw frozen package, add water, stir, warm and serve.

Red-Eye Ham

I love ham slices for travel days. You can buy them in most grocery stores, they hold up well, and they are easy to heat up and eat. I do like a little extra flavor though and this recipe easily provides just that.

SERVES [2]

INGREDIENTS

4 slices thick precooked ham
3/4 cup brewed black coffee (you can use decaf if you are worried about the caffeine)
1 tsp granulated sugar

DIRECTIONS

1. Heat a few drops of oil in a large skillet until the skillet is medium hot.
2. Sear on one side for 30 seconds flip and then sear the other side.
3. Add coffee to the pan.
3. Simmer on low heat until warmed. Do not over cook.
4. Sprinkle with sugar and stir.
5. Serve

Easy and Delicious Baked Fish

When I started trying new recipes this was the very first recipe good enough to make my web page, Very easy to make, relatively

SERVES [2]

INGREDIENTS

1 cup herb season stuffing mix; finely crushed
4 TBL butter; melted
One 7.6 oz pkg of grill flavored frozen fish
2 tsp lemon juice

DIRECTIONS

1. Preheat oven to 425°.
2. Combine stuffing with butter. Toss well until mixed.
3. Lightly grease a baking dish.
4. Place fish in dish and sprinkle with with lemon juice.
5. Place crumb mixture lightly on fish placing extra around the sides.
6. Bake in preheated oven for 18-20 minutes or until fish flakes easily with a fork.
7. Serve.

All American Hamburger

Hamburgers are an easy travel day meal and this recipe uses a few common ingredients to quickly improve the flavor

SERVES [2]

INGREDIENTS

1 lb ground beef
1 tsp Worcester sauce
1/2 tsp onion powder
1/2 tsp seasoning salt
1/4 tsp pepper

DIRECTIONS

1. Combine all ingredients in a bowl and mix well.
2. Form four 4" patties.
3. Grill or cook in a pan for 10 minutes; turning once.
4. Serve with your favorite condiments and sides.

Cinnamon Oranges

Need something sweet and easy to snack on when traveling?
This recipe is great for rest stops on a hot day.

SERVES [2]

INGREDIENTS

3 oranges; peeled and thinly sliced crosswise
1/4 sugar
1/4 tsp ground cinnamon

DIRECTIONS

1. Peel and slice oranges.
2, Place slices in one layer in a serving dish.
2. Mix sugar and cinnamon in a separate dish.
3. Sprinkle sugar/cinnamon mixture over first layer of orange slices.
4. Add a second layer of slices and sprinkle with mix.
5. Cover and place in refrigerator for at least one hour.
6. Serve and enjoy.

Chicken and Stuffing Bake

I tried several chicken and stuffing recipes, and we definitely liked this one the best. It's simple enough to cook on a travel day.

SERVES [4]

INGREDIENTS

4 TBL margarine; melted
4 cups dry stuffing mix
4 - 6 boneless chicken thighs
Paprika
One 10-3/4 oz can of cream of mushroom soup
1/3 cup milk
1 TBL minced parsley

DIRECTIONS

1. Preheat oven to 400°.
2. In a bowl combine water, melted butter, and stuffing mix; stir well.
3. Spoon stuffing lengthwise down the middle of a 13 x 9 baking dish.
4. Arrange chicken pieces on each side of the line of stuffing.
5. Sprinkle with paprika
6. In a bowl combine soup, milk, and parsley then pour over chicken.
7. Cover and bake for 30 minutes or until chicken is done.
8. Serve.

Fried Rice

I love fried rice and it's easy to throw together on travel days. We tried several recipes, but nothing was quite right until I combined several ingredients and made my own.

SERVE [2]

INGREDIENTS

4 TBL peanut or corn oil
4 cups day old cooked rice
4 green onions; sliced thin
1/2 to 3/4 cup diced ham, chicken, or pork
2 TBL soy sauce
2 eggs

DIRECTIONS

1. Heat the oil in a skillet or wok.
2. Beat eggs in separate dish.
3. Add rice to wok and cook for 5 minutes stirring frequently.
4. Add egg and 1/2 sliced green onion.
5. Stir until eggs are set.
6. Serve; garnish with remaining green onions

Mom's Spaghetti Sauce

If my family has a recipe legacy this is it. This sauce came from my mother who got it from my grandmother and I have loved it since childhood. I taught my three girls how to make it and it makes my day when they occasionally call me to make sure they got the recipe right.

I wasn't sure if this would work well in an RV, but I make a large batch and freeze it in smaller portions. Perfect for a travel day or any day I don't feel like going to much trouble.

SERVE [12]

INGREDIENTS

3 lbs hamburger
Three 32 oz cans tomato sauce
Three 12 oz cans tomato paste
3 TBL onion salt
3 TBL garlic salt
4 TBL oregano or Italian seasoning
3 TBL Parmesan cheese
3 tsp sugar
1 tsp salt
1 tsp pepper

DIRECTIONS

1. Brown the ground beef; drain grease.
2. Place tomato sauce and tomato paste in large pot.
3. Fill empty tomato paste cans with water and let stand.
4. Add all seasonings to tomato sauce and stir *well*.
5. Add water and any remaining tomato paste from cans.
6. Stir until tomato paste is smooth.
7. Add hamburger to sauce.
8. Mix sauce thoroughly with a large slotted spoon.
9. Bring sauce to a light boil then simmer; stirring frequently to ensure sauce does not burn.
10. Remove from heat, cool, and let sit over night.
11. Separate sauce into two meal portions then freeze.

Kelly's Baked Potato Soup

A hearty soup can be a great travel day meal and this is the very best potato soup I have ever had. It lasts for several days in the fridge, but add some milk and stir prior to heating up.

SERVES [8]

INGREDIENTS

6 large russet potatoes
2/3 cup <u>real</u> butter
2/3 cup flour
1-1/2 quarts of milk
1 cup sour cream
2 cups cooked bacon; crumbled or use real bacon bits
1 cup shredded cheese; mild cheddar or Monterey jack/ Colby blend
4 green onions; thinly sliced
salt and pepper

DIRECTIONS

1. Bake potatoes in a 350° oven until fork tender.
2. When done cooking set aside to cool.
3. When cool cut 4 potatoes in half and scoop out insides. Mash them.
4. Peel the other two potatoes and cut into chunks.
5. Melt butter in a medium saucepan. Slowly blend in flour with a wire whisk until thoroughly blended.(Roux).
6. Gradually add the milk to the roux, whisking constantly; sprinkle with salt and pepper. Keep mixture simmering as you add milk.
7. While milk mixture is hot whisk in mashed potatoes. If soup is too thick you can add a little extra milk.
8. Mix in 3/4 of the green onion, all of the sour cream, 1/2 the bacon, and potato chunks. Heat thoroughly.
9. Serve soup sprinkled with remaining bacon green onions, and cheese.

Wannabe Big Don Sub

One of the things we miss the most about traveling is being able to get a Big Don Sub® from Donatos Pizza®. After much trial and error this recipe gets us close to the real thing. The Marzetti Dressing packets are hard to find but really are the key.

SERVES [1]

INGREDIENTS

One packet Marzetti's House Italian Dressing®
If you absolutely have to substitute choose a very tart Italian dressing
4 slices salami
4 slices ham
4 slices pepperoni
1 large deli slice
1 slice provolone cheese; cut in half
<u>Shredded</u> lettuce
shredding definitely makes a difference
2 <u>Roma</u> tomato slices
has to be Roma
Banana pepper slices
optional
One <u>seedless</u> sub roll

DIRECTIONS

1. Preheat stove on broiler setting.
3. Place both pieces of roll cut side down on a cookie sheet greased with cooking spray.
4. Place cookie sheet on bottom of RV oven <u>under</u> the propane flame for 2 minutes until tops are cooked slightly but not burnt.
5. On bottom pieces of roll place <u>in order</u> 1/4 packet salad dressing, ham, salami, pepperoni, and cheese.
6. Place bottoms back under broiler for 2-3 minutes until edges of bread are brown and cheese is bubbling.
7. Place 1/4 packet of dressing on top bun then lettuce, tomato slices, and peppers if desired. Top with remaining dressing.
8. Place sandwich halves together and heat under broiler for roughly 1 minute.
9. Slice in half at a diagonal and enjoy!!

Pressure Cooker

••

Almost every RVer I know has a slow cooker because there is nothing better than putting a meal on early in the morning, seeings the sights all day, and then coming home to a hot meal. Unfortunately, I found that I wasn't that great at planning ahead so rarely used mine. That all changed when I purchased an Instantpot®. This high pressure cooker not only significantly reduced the time needed for a "slow cooked" meal, but could also cook frozen meat. Perfect for someone like me who are constantly forgetting to take something out of the freezer for dinner. Most of these recipes will work in a slow cooker as well as a pressure cooker, they just take a little longer.

Super Easy Chicken

Sometimes you want something simple yet tasty and this certainly fits the bill. Perfect for a day you forgot to take anything out of the freezer

Serves [2]

Ingredients

4 frozen chicken thighs
1 cup chicken broth
1 packet Good Seasons Italian Dressing®

Directions

1. Place chicken in slow cooker or pressure cooker.
2. Sprinkle packet of seasoning on chicken.
3. Add chicken broth.
4. Slow cook for several hours until juices run clear or cook for 15 minutes on high pressure setting.
5. Serve.

Cori's Shredded Pork

I tried several different recipes for shredded pork but none tasted as good as Cori's. It's really simple, but draining the grease is absolutely the key. We love eating this for lunch on travel days because it heats up so well in the microwave.

SERVES [8]

INGREDIENTS

3-4 lbs of pork loin
1-2 bottles BBQ sauce
Water

DIRECTIONS

1. Put pork in a crock pot with some water and 1/3 bottle BBQ sauce for 4-5 hours
2. Drain grease
3. Shred pork and add remainder of one bottle of sauce. Add additional to consistency desired
4. Cook additional time as needed to soften pork
5. Serve on buns. Freezes well and heats very well in microwave.

Baked Potatoes

I was a little skeptical that this would work, but they really cook pretty fast and taste great. If you need some extra softness, pop in the microwave for 5 minutes or for a crunchy skin finish off in oven at 400° for 15 minutes.

SERVES [2]

INGREDIENTS

Idaho Baking Potatoes

DIRECTIONS

1. Place trivet in bottom of pressure cooker and add water to right below the potatoes.
2. Poke several holes in potato with knife then place in pressure cooker.
3. Cook on High Pressure for 15 minutes.
4. Use quick release to remove steam.

Caramel and Apples

This is one of Lee's favorite recipes but dipping caramel can be expensive. Not only is this a yummier alternative, but it also is less expensive. Try substituting chocolate evaporated milk for a chocolate dip.

SERVES [4]

INGREDIENTS

One can of sweetened condensed milk
Apples

DIRECTIONS

1. Place can (without wrapper) in pressure cooker on the metal basket or in a metal strainer. Do not allow the can to touch base or sides of pressure cooker.
2. Fill with water until at 1/2 mark of can.
3. Cook on High Pressure for 15 minutes.
4. Allow to depressurize naturally; do NOT use quick release.
5. Let stand for several hours until completely cool. Do not open until can is no longer warm.
6. Open can and serve with sliced apples.

Fruited Rice

This was one of those recipes that I tried once and couldn't get out of my mind. Luckily I held onto the recipe and was able to adapt it for the pressure cooker.

SERVES [4]

INGREDIENTS

2 cups water
1 TBL butter
1 tsp salt
1 cup enriched white rice
3 TBL golden raisins
8 oz can mandarin oranges ;drained and chopped
2 oz sliced almonds
Cooking spray

DIRECTIONS

1. Spray the inside of pressure cooker pan with butter flavored cooking spray.
2. Rinse rice in strainer.
3. Add rice, water, and salt to pressure cooker.
4. Stir.
5. Cook on high pressure for 12 minutes.
6. Use quick release to open pressure cooker.
7. Add oranges, almonds, and raisins to rice and stir.
8. Serve.

Pressure Cooker Lasagna

Lee loves lasagna but it always seems like too much work for me, so imagine my excitement when I figured out a way to make it in the pressure cooker. You can use any lasagna recipe, just make sure to use oven ready noodles. , I have just provided a very simple recipe below

SERVES [4]

INGREDIENTS

One 26 oz jar of meat sauce
5-6 sheets of <u>oven ready</u> lasagna noodles
1/2# of mozzarella; sliced
1/4 # grated or shredded fresh Parmesan cheese
Olive oil cooking spray

DIRECTIONS

1. Spray the inside of the pressure cooker/slow cooker with cooking spray.
2. Using a large spoon spread a thin layer of sauce over the bottom of the crock or insert.
3. Use lasagna pieces to cover the sauce. You can break the pieces as needed to fill in the gaps.
4. Lightly cover the noodles with sauce.
5. Sprinkle noodles with a layer of mozzarella cheese.
6. Repeat steps 2-5 until you run out of sauce making sure the top layer is sauce.
7. Sprinkle Parmesan cheese on top.
8. Cook on high pressure for 10 minutes.
9. Use quick release to remove steam and turn off cooker. Let sit for an 10 additional minutes.
If using a slow cooker cook on HIGH for 3-1/2 hours then test for noodle tenderness.
10. Using a spatula gently work the lasagna pie from the sides and then cut into triangle shaped pieces.
11. Serve.

Golden Beef Stew

Lee and I both love beef stew but we never could find a recipe we both liked. One night we created this one together and we both think it's pretty yummy.

SERVES [4]

INGREDIENTS

2 lbs cubed stew meat
4 large potatoes peeled and cubed
4 large carrots sliced and cubed
8 oz sliced mushrooms
1 large onion chopped
1 envelope onion soup mix
2 cans golden mushroom soup

DIRECTIONS

1. Place potatoes, carrots, and onion in pressure cooker or crock pot.
2. Spread stew meat over vegetables.
3. Put mushrooms on top of stew meat.
4. Combine 2 cups of water with onion soup mix then add two cans of golden mushroom soup; stir well.
5. Pour mixture on top of mushrooms.
6. Cook on high pressure for 30 minutes or cook on low pressure for 5-6 hours.
7. Stir then serve with biscuits or hearty bread. Salt and pepper each bowl to taste.

Lee Finally Likes It Pot Roast

I love roast but Lee is not a fan because he feels it rarely has any flavor. After numerous tries he declared this recipe to be the best pot roast he had ever had.

SERVES [4]

INGREDIENTS

3 lb boneless chuck roast; well marbled
1 TBL canola oil
1-1/2 cups water
1/2 tsp garlic powder
1/2 tsp pepper
1 envelope brown gravy mix
1 envelope onion soup mix
1 envelope Good Seasons Italian salad dressing mix®
5-6 medium potatoes
3-4 carrots

DIRECTIONS

1. Lightly brown roast in canola oil on all sides then place meat in pressure cooker/crock pot.
2. In small bowl combine water, garlic powder, gravy, Italian dressing, and onion soup mix; whisk until blended.
3. Pour mixture over meat.
4. Cook on high pressure for 35 minutes or cook on low pressure for three hours.
5. Skim fat if necessary.
6. Add potatoes and carrots on top of meat then cook on high pressure for an additional 35 minutes or cook on low pressure for 2-3 more hours until meat and vegetables are tender.

Chinese Pot Roast Chicken

This recipe is a result of adapting a stove top recipe to the pressure cooker. It is also the first time I ever cooked with sherry and I was surprised by how much a tablespoon impacted the flavors. It's several steps but definitely worth it.

SERVES [4]

INGREDIENTS

3 lb chicken thighs
1/4 cup + 2 TBL low-salt soy sauce
2 TBL vegetable oil
1 TBL cooking sherry
1 clove garlic; minced
2 stalks celery; cut in 1" pieces
6 whole mushrooms; cut into 6ths
3 green onions; cut into 1" pieces
3/4 cup water
1 TBL cornstarch
1 tsp sugar

DIRECTIONS

1. Rinse chicken and pat dry with paper towels.
2. Rub chicken thoroughly with 1/4 cup soy sauce; allow to stand at least 15 minutes.
3. Saute oil and minced garlic in pressure cooker for 1-2 minutes.
4. Add cooking sherry.
5. Add chicken and cook on high pressure for 15 minutes.
6. Use quick release valve to open lid.
7. Remove chicken with slotted spoon and set aside.
8. Add celery, mushrooms, and green onions and saute for one to two minutes.
9. Combine water, 2 TBL soy sauce, and cornstarch in a separate bowl and mix well then add to pot.
10. Saute for 10-15 minutes; stirring frequently, until sauce thickens.
11. Add chicken back into sauce and mix well.
12. Serve with rice.

Clam Chowder

When looking for the perfect recipe often I will cook several variations and determine our favorite. Once in awhile though none seem quite right so I will take my favorite components of each and come up with something new. This recipe is the combination of five different clam chowder recipes and I was really happy with the final result.

Serves [4]

Ingredients

One 16 oz can potatoes; chopped
2 small cans chopped clams with juice
3 TBL flour
1/4 tsp salt
Dash pepper
1 pint half and half cream
2 tsp parsley
3 TBL real butter
1/3 medium onion; chopped fine
Oyster Crackers

Directions

1. Spray the inside of the pressure cooker with nonstick cooking spray.
2. Put melted butter in pan and whisk in flour to make a roux.
3. Stir in half and half.
4. Add clams (with juice); onion, salt, pepper, and parsley then stir.
5. Cook on high pressure for 15 minutes and then allow to simmer until natural release is complete; approximately 30-45 minutes total.
6. Serve with oyster crackers.

Dinners for Two

After many years of cooking for a family of five it was tough to adjust to cooking for just two people. But we quickly got tired of throwing food away, so I learned to scale the meals down. Most of these meals are sized for two people, but they almost always have leftovers. They are also pretty easy to scale up if you are feeding 4-6 people.

Spicy Drumsticks with Blue Cheese

I love hot wings but never thought about using it for a main dish. The combination of grill flavor and hot sauce makes these delicious and dipping the chicken into blue cheese is also fun

SERVES [2]

INGREDIENTS

4 chicken drumsticks
3 TBL vegetable Oil
3 TBL white vinegar
4 tsp red pepper sauce
3/4 tsp salt

DIRECTIONS

1. Mix oil, vinegar, pepper sauce, and salt in Ziploc® plastic bag
2. Add drumsticks and toss until well coated.
3. Refrigerate at least 1 hour;occasionally turning bag.
4. Cook chicken on grill for 30 minutes; save remaining sauce in bag.
5. Baste chicken with remaining sauce and then cook an additional 10-15 minutes.
6. Serve with blue cheese dressing for dipping sauce.

Sirloin Tips and Noodles

I created this recipe when the kids were small because it was a great way to stretch a cheaper piece of beef. The kids still love it and I do too. The leftovers heat up well if you put a wet napkin over the noodles before microwaving.

SERVES [2]

INGREDIENTS

2 lb of any grilling steak
1/4 -1/2 cup butter
One 12 oz package wide egg noodles
Garlic salt
1 large can of sliced or button mushrooms

DIRECTIONS

1. Broil, grill, or pan fry steak to medium rare.
2. Cut meat into bite size pieces and set aside.
3. Boil egg noodles per package directions; drain.
4. Place mushrooms and 1/4 cup butter in pan, sauce pan.
5. Sprinkle with garlic salt and cook on medium-low heat until mushrooms are lightly browned.
6. Add steak to mushrooms and saute until steak is desired doneness.
7. Combine noodles, steak, mushrooms and butter sauce in a pot and heat for a few minutes on medium low until all ingredients are hot.
8. Add more butter and garlic salt to taste.
9. Serve

Crazy Marinade Pork Chops

When I first found this recipe I thought no way would this taste good . Too many ingredients and I am not a big fan of pork chops. But Lee loves them so I gave it a try. Wow, what a pleasant surprise. This is the only pork chop recipe that I have found that I actually like because the meat is flavorful and moist.

SERVES [2]

INGREDIENTS

3/4 cup canola oil
1/3 cup soy sauce
1/4 cup white vinegar
2 TBL Worcestershire sauce
1 TBL lemon juice
1 TBL prepared yellow mustard
1 tsp salt
1 tsp pepper
1 tsp dried parsley flakes
1 garlic clove; minced
4 pork chops

DIRECTIONS

1. Combine all ingredients (except pork) and blend well.
2. Place pork in large Ziploc® bag. Add marinade and shake to mix well.
3. Place in refrigerator overnight.
4. Drain and discard marinade.
5. Grill covered over medium heat; 4 minutes per side.
6. Let stand 5 minutes before serving.

Coffee-Rubbed Flank Steak

I tried numerous recipes for London Broil before Lee finally approved this one. He is a fan of rib eye and not crazy about any lesser cut of meat, but this is so flavorful that he actually said he liked it.

SERVES [4]

INGREDIENTS

1/4 lb flank steak
1 TBL finely ground coffee
1 TBL light brown sugar; packed
1-1/2 tsp chili powder
1-1/2 tsp dried ginger
1-1/2 tsp paprika
1 tsp kosher salt
1/2 tsp cayenne pepper

DIRECTIONS

1. Combine all ingredients (except steak) in a small bowl and blend well.
2. Rub coffee and spice mixture onto one side of flank steak; shake off excess when complete.
3. Turn steak over and repeat
4. Oil grill grates then preheat grill to high.
5. Cook for 3-1/2 minutes then turn over and cook for another 3-1/2 minutes.
6. Let steak rest for 5 full minutes before slicing.
7. Cut steak in thin strips at a diagonal.
8. Serve with juices.

Smothered Chicken

When we were in Alaska and I was working 11-8 Lee was cooking dinner every night. I gave him some recipes to try and this was by far his favorite. Why? Bacon!

SERVES [2]

INGREDIENTS

4 boneless chicken thighs
Garlic powder
1 TBL vegetable oil
4 oz of sliced mushrooms (fresh or canned; drained)
1 cup (4 oz) Mexican shredded cheese blend
1/2 cup chopped green onions
1/2 cup bacon bits
Lawry's seasoning salt

DIRECTIONS

1. If desired flatten chicken to 1/4" thickness (*Lee skipped this step and it still tasted great*).
2. Sprinkle chicken with garlic powder and seasoning salt.
3. Brown chicken in oil for 4 minutes over medium heat in large, nonstick skillet. Drain grease.
4. Top chicken with mushrooms, cheese, green onions, and bacon.
5. Cover and cook until juices run clear and cheese is melted; about 4 minutes.

Skillet Chicken

This dish was a result of trying to use up what we had lying around the house. To be honest I didn't expect much once it was done, but this is one of those recipes where every bite tastes better than the last.

SERVES [2]

INGREDIENTS

4 boneless chicken thighs
2 TBL olive oil
1 can diced tomatoes
1 jar (4 oz) sliced mushrooms; drained
1 clove garlic; minced
1 envelope Lipton Onion soup mix®
Pasta

DIRECTIONS

1. In a large skillet heat oil and brown chicken; drain grease from pan.
2. Combine tomatoes, mushrooms, garlic and soup mix.
3. Stir mixture in with chicken.
4. Cover and simmer for 30-45 minutes until chicken is tender.
5. Serve over pasta.

Crunchy Fried Dill Fish

I am usually not a fan of fried fish, but this has a nice crunchy coat and the inside is moist but not greasy.

SERVES [2]

INGREDIENTS

1 lb thick fish fillets
1/2 cup water
2 TBL lemon juice
1 cup finely crushed Tollhouse Cracker® crumbs
1 tsp salt
1 tsp dried dill weed
1/4 tsp pepper
1 egg; beaten
Vegetable Oil for frying

DIRECTIONS

1. Fill skillet with 1/4" - 1/2" oil.
2. Cut pieces of fish (if needed) so they will lay flat in pan.
3. Soak fish fillets in lemon juice and water in a large Ziploc bag®.
4. Combine cracker crumbs with salt, pepper, and dill weed. Mix well.
5. Beat eggs in a separate container.
6. Drain fish and pat dry.
7. Dredge fish in egg and coating until covered.
8. Fry in hot oil 3 minutes on each side.
9. Serve.

Grandma Betty's Meatloaf

This is the first recipe that my grandmother shared with me after I got married. It's one of Lee's favorites and I have been making it our entire marriage. Plus. it always makes me feel closer to her when I make it.

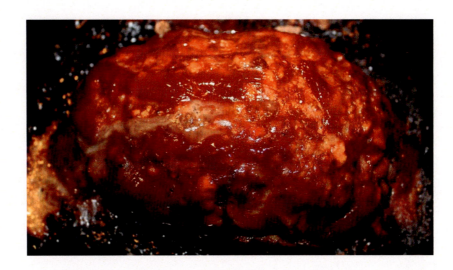

SERVES [4]

INGREDIENTS

2 lb hamburger
1 egg
1 cup crumbled saltine crackers
1/2 cup milk
1 package Lipton's onion soup mix®

Basting Sauce
1 cup ketchup
1/2 cup BBQ sauce

DIRECTIONS

1. Place hamburger in a large mixing bowl and add soup mix, crackers, milk, and egg.
2. In a separate small bowl mix ketchup and BBQ sauce.
3. Preheat oven to 350°.
4. Mix hamburger and ingredients VERY well using your hands.
5. Shape mixture into a loaf in a baking pan.
6. Brush meatloaf with 1/2 of the sauce; save remainder for second basting.
7. Cover pan.
8. Cook 1/2 hour at 350°.
9. Drain grease; baste with remaining sauce; cover and put back in oven.
10. Cook an additional 1/2 hour.
11. Remove from oven and cut down the middle; push two halves apart.
12. Place in oven for an additional 10 -15 minutes uncovered until top is lightly browned.
13. Serve.

Daddy's Special Chicken

Lee learned this recipe from his stepfather Denny and we all loved it when he made it for us.   It's time consuming but so very good. For this recipe, Lee wrote the steps.

SERVES [4]

INGREDIENTS

4 Chicken breasts or thighs (boneless/skinless)
Real butter
Lemon juice
Flour
Garlic salt and pepper

DIRECTIONS

1. Cut the chicken into small portions; about 3" square
2. Pound it as thin as you can get it. The thinner the better. It helps to pound them between sheets of plastic wrap, or between cocktails.
3. In a frying pan, melt butter and get the pan as hot as you can without the butter smoking.
4. Dredge damp chicken in flour.
5. Sprinkle it with Garlic salt, pepper, lemon juice and fry only until the coating gets crispy and brown.
6. Turn only once, and sprinkle again with garlic salt, pepper and lemon juice, and fry the other side.
7. Once they are cooked, keep them warm in the oven
8. Eat as many as you can before other people can get any!
9. Make someone else clean up the mess.

Crab Stuffed Cod

This is one of my favorite New England meals that I tried for years to duplicate and finally managed to while we were visiting Louisiana. The key is good fish and real crab meat which is very easy to find there.

SERVES [4]

INGREDIENTS

4 pieces Cod, Sole, Haddock, or Flounder fillets
1 cup soft bread crumbs
1 cup fresh crab meat
1 small yellow onion; finely chopped
1 egg; lightly beaten
1/2 tsp salt
Dash cayenne pepper
3 TBL butter ; melted and divided
1 TBL flour
1/2 cup chicken broth (low sodium)
Grated Parmesan cheese *from the deli*

DIRECTIONS

1. In a bowl combine bread crumbs. crab, onion, egg, salt, and cayenne pepper.
2. Mix well.
3. Spoon onto middle of underside of fillet then roll both ends up and secure with two wooden skewers.
4. Bake at 375°; uncovered for 25-30 minutes in a greased pan until fish flakes easily with a fork; drizzle with 2 TBL of butter prior to baking.
5. Place remaining butter in a saucepan, stir in flour until smooth. Gradually add broth, stirring and cook and stir for 2 minutes until thick and bubbly.
6. Drain liquid from baking dish and then spoon sauce over fillets.
7. Put Parmesan cheese on fillets and broil for 3-5 minutes until cheese is melted and lightly browned.
8. Remove skewers and serve.

Side Dishes

One of my favorite parts of traveling, is shopping at local farmer's markets. Cooking with local, fresh ingredients is amazing. Almost all of these side dishes will taste best with fresh ingredients, but frozen or canned can also be substituted in some cases. I think vegetables should be the star, so most of these recipes are simple, with flavors designed to enhance rather than mask the fresh flavors.

Easy Peasy Green Beans

As much as I love fresh green beans you can't always find them, so I have been making green beans from the can this way since I was a kid

SERVES [2]

INGREDIENTS

Can of French cut green beans
Margarine
Garlic Salt

DIRECTIONS

1. Drain green beans from can.
2. Place in skillet with 1/4 cup margarine.
3. Sprinkle with garlic salt.
4. Cook on medium heat stirring occasionally for 15-20 minutes, until slightly crisp.
5. Serve.

Sesame Scented Snow Pea Pods

Lightly cooked snow pea pods are still crunchy and the sesame oil gives them just the right amount of seasoning while still allowing their flavor to shine through

SERVES [2]

INGREDIENTS

1/2 lb fresh snow pea pods
1/2 tsp sesame oil

DIRECTIONS

1. Steam snow pea pods for 3 minutes until bright green but still crisp.
2. Drain snow peas and pat dry.
3. Place in bowl and toss lightly with sesame oil. If you have spray oil this works great. Squirt 3 times then toss then 3-4 times.
4. Serve immediately.

Bacon Wrapped Corn on the Cob

Who doesn't like fresh corn? Add bacon and it is sure to be a crowd pleaser!

SERVES [4]

INGREDIENTS

4 ears of fresh corn
4 bacon strips
 2 TBL chili powder

DIRECTIONS

1. Husk the corn and place on a large piece of foil.
2. Wrap corn in a piece of bacon.
3. Sprinkle with chili powder.
4. Close the corn in foil and cook over medium heat for 20 minutes.
5. Flip once after 10 minutes
6. Unwrap and serve.

Baby Carrots with Fresh Dill

I'm not a huge fan of cooked carrots but these retain enough of their crunch and carrot flavor to make them tasted good Plus they are pretty.

SERVES [4]

INGREDIENTS

12 oz baby carrots
2 TBL butter; *melted*
Fresh dill

DIRECTIONS

1. Cook baby carrots in boiling water until tender 10-15 minutes.
2. Drain carrots and place in serving bowl.
3. Add melted butter and toss until carrots are coated.
4. Place snipped fresh dill sprigs on dish.

Petits Pois

I like peas but it's nice when they have a little extra. The peanut oil and onion really add something, but you can still taste the peas.

Serves [2]

Ingredients

3 TBL peanut oil
2 cups tiny fresh peas or 10 oz frozen petite peas
1/4 cup chopped onion
1/2 tsp salt
1/4 tsp pepper

Directions

1. Heat peanut oil in a skillet.
2. Add peas, onion, salt and pepper and cook. over medium heat for 5-10 minutes until done; stir frequently.
3. Serve.

Deb's Tiny Potatoes

My friend Deb can cook. I mean throw things in a pot, stir a little, and amazing food comes out cook. Thankfully for me this recipe was simple enough that I could duplicate it.

Serves [4]

Ingredients

Small bag of white or red new potatoes
1 stick of real butter
Parsley
Salt

Directions

1. Boil potatoes in salt water until fork tender.
2. Drain.
3. Add 1/2 to 1 stick of butter (use generously).
4. Season with parsley.
5. Serve.

Skillet Fresh Green Beans

I love fresh green beans and have tried many recipes, but this is by far my favorite. They are lightly flavored and the beans are crunchy!

SERVES [4]

INGREDIENTS

1 lb of fresh green beans
4 TBL real butter
4-6 garlic cloves, thinly sliced
Salt
Sugar
1/2 cup water

DIRECTIONS

1. Melt butter in large skillet over medium-high heat.
2. Add thinly sliced garlic cloves and cook; stir frequently for 2 minutes.
3. Add trimmed green beans and a few pinches of sugar and salt; cook 2 minutes.
4. Add 1/2 cup water, cover, cook until tender about 6 minutes.
5. Uncover and boil until the water mostly evaporates about 1-2 minutes.
6. Serve.

Tomatoes Vinaigrette

A really good tomato doesn't need anything, but those aren't always available.
This is a great way to dress up a hothouse tomato.

SERVES [2]

INGREDIENTS

4 very thick tomato slices
Minced red onion; red (instant,
Parsley flakes
Good Seasons® Italian Salad Dressing

DIRECTIONS

1. Arrange thick tomato slices in square container.
2. Cover with salad dressing.
3. Sprinkle with onion and parsley.
4. Cover and refrigerate for 3 hours basting occasionally.
5. Serve immediately.

Fried Carrot Chips

I am a huge fan of competition cooking shows, but am not a good enough cook at this point to make most of the food I see. This recipe though was easy enough that I could make it and with some slight variation I thought it tasted great.

SERVES [2]

INGREDIENTS

Peanut or Canola Oil for frying
4 large carrots
1 TBL cornstarch

DIRECTIONS

1. Fill a deep fryer or large sauce pan halfway with oil and bring temperature to between 350 and 365°.
2. Slice carrots diagonally making 1/4 inch slices.
3. Toss in cornstarch.
4. Fry for 3 minutes until crispy but not brown.
5. Serve.

Fried Potatoes

I learned this recipe many years ago when I worked at Denny's®
and my favorite cook used to make them for me. A bit messy to cook, but worth it.

SERVES [4]

INGREDIENTS

6 Idaho baking potatoes
Vegetable Oil
3-4 green onions

DIRECTIONS

1. Peel potatoes and slice thin.
2. Place 1-2 inches of oil in deep pan and heat to popping.
3. Carefully place potato slices in pan then cover.
4. Cook 20 minutes on medium heat, turning frequently so they are lightly browned but not burned.
5. Remove potatoes and pat dry with paper towel.
6. Drain oil from pan.
7. Place potatoes back in pan and toss quickly with chopped green onions. *Onions should be slightly warm on outside but crunchy and cool on inside.*
8. Serve.

Regional Specialties

One of my favorite things about cooking in an RV has been experimenting with different regional recipes. Some of the ingredients can be a little harder to find, but we stock up in our travels when we run across a local specialty grocery store. Finding space for extra ingredients can be a little challenging, but with some menu planning I think it's totally worth it for the variety. The one piece of special cooking equipment I use to make some of these dishes is a wok. If you don't have one you can easily substitute a large, deep skillet.

Easy Stuffed Shells

While in Quartzsite one winter we were all comparing recipes with under 5 ingredients and Pam said this was one of her favorites. We tried it and agreed.

SERVES [4]

INGREDIENTS

16 uncooked pasta shells
16 oz meatless spaghetti sauce
16 frozen fully cooked Italian meatballs; thawed
1-2 cups shredded mozzarella cheese

DIRECTIONS

1. Thaw meatballs.
2. Cook pasta shells as directed by the box, drain, and rinse with cool water.
3. Preheat oven to 350°
4. Place 1/2 cup sauce in bottom of a baking dish.
5. Place one thawed meatball inside each shell and lay shells on top of sauce.
6. Pour remaining sauce over shells.
7. Sprinkle with cheese.
8. Bake covered for 35 minutes.
9. Uncover and bake for 3-7 minutes until cheese is melted and bubbly.
10. Serve 4 shells per portion.

Spicy Korean Pork

Lee is a fan of spicy pork dishes and I experimented with several recipes until I finally found one that was simple enough for me to make and not too spicy. Recommend serving with brown rice.

SERVES [2]

INGREDIENTS

2 lb country-style boneless pork ribs; cut into one inch cubes
2 TBL chili garlic sauce
1/2 cup soy sauce
2 tsp ginger
2 TBL sesame oil
3 TBL brown sugar
Brown Rice

DIRECTIONS

1. Add all ingredients (except pork) and whisk into a blended marinade.
2. Add cubed pork to the mix and let sit for at least 20 minutes.
3. Grilled marinated pork (you can place on skewers if that is easier), uncovered for 10 minutes turning every 2-3 minutes.
4. Serve on rice.

Chicken Fingers Italiano

Every one in awhile I try a simple recipe and it turns out to taste amazing. This definitely fell into that category with only a few ingredients and an absolutely yummy taste.

Serves [2]

Ingredients

4 chicken thighs or breasts
1 cup Italian breadcrumbs
2 eggs
1 cup olive oil for frying
Marinara sauce (or Connie's spaghetti sauce with no meat)

Directions

1. Cut chicken into thin strips.
2. Warm marinara sauce.
3. Beat eggs in a bowl.
4. Place breadcrumbs in separate bowl.
5. Dip chicken in egg mixture then in breadcrumbs to coat.
6. Place <u>olive oil</u> in a large deep skillet. Place over medium high heat until a drop of water in skillet "pops" Do not substitute oil type.
7. Cook chicken until browned on both sides turning a few times; 4-6 minutes depending on thickness of slice.
8. Serve with warm marinara sauce for dipping and some spaghetti (with marinara) on the side.

Satay Pork

This pork recipe is flavorful but not spicy, plus the skewer sticks are fun. If you don't have them you can cook the pork on a grill mat, but it is not as fun to eat.

Serves [4]

Ingredients

3 lb boneless pork cut into strips
1/2 cup vegetable oil
1/4 cup soy sauce
2 TBL chopped peanuts
1 TBL Worcestershire Sauce
1 TBL chopped onion
2 cloves garlic; crushed
2 tsp brown sugar
1/4 tsp curry powder
Wooden Skewers (optional)

Directions

1. Combine all ingredients except pork; blend well.
2. Marinate pork for 1-2 hours; stir occasionally.
3. Drain pork; reserve marinade.
4. Thread pork onto skewers in a "S" pattern.
5. Grill kabobs on an uncovered grill for 5-6 minutes turning frequently and marinating often.
6. Serve.

Grilled Pizza

This recipe can be made on your grill or over a campfire. It is very simple but creates gourmet pizza flavors . If a nearby grocery store has a salad bar, check it out to pick up some reasonably priced toppings.

SERVES [4]

INGREDIENTS

1 roll of Pillsbury Pizza Crust®
15 oz pizza sauce
Mozzarella Cheese
Olive oil
Toppings as desired

DIRECTIONS

1. Heat the grill making sure it is clean of any residue.
2. Open the roll and lay the pizza dough on a flat surface.
3. Cut to the desired size
4. Using an old towel folded and held with tongs oil the grill with olive oil
5. Lay pizza dough flat on the grill
6. Cook for 2-3 minutes until underside is marked and top side is bubbling a little (do not walk away from the grill as this must be closely monitored)
7. Flip the dough and cook an additional 2-3 minutes on the other side
8. Remove dough to a cookie sheet
9. Place pizza sauce on the dough and top as desired. Lightly portion the toppings
10. Place pizza on a griddle covering with foil and ensuring the foil does not touch the cheese
11. Place back on the fire cooking for 3-5 minutes until cheese is melted (again closely monitor)
12. Plate and serve

Stir Fry

I love stir fry but none of the recipes were quite right. After trying recipe after recipe this one is close to what I was looking for. You can use beef, pork, or shrimp as the meat.

SERVES [4]

INGREDIENTS

1 lb lean pork
2 TBL vegetable oil
3 cloves <u>real</u> garlic; minced
4 TBL low salt soy sauce
2 TBL sherry
8 oz rice noodles
1 small head broccoli
5-6 mushrooms
4 oz snow pea pods

DIRECTIONS

1. Cut pork into thin strips.
2. Combine sherry and soy sauce; stir.
3. Heat oil then add minced garlic. Saute for 1-2 minutes.
4. Add pork and stir fry for 2-3 minutes making sure pork is browned.
5. Add 1/2 sherry/soy sauce mix.
6. Allow pork to simmer; stir frequently.
7. Add broccoli and mushrooms. Stir fry for 2-3 minutes.
8. Add noodles and pour remaining sauce on top then stir for 2-3 minutes.
9. Add snow pea pods. Stir 1-2 minutes.
10. Serve.

Crunchy Baked Chimichangas

These chimis actually get nice and crunchy in the oven and the cumin really adds something special to the flavor. Lee says they taste really close to Chi-Chi's® chimichangas and they pair great with Kelly's Queso Dip and chips.

Serves [4]

Ingredients

1-1/2 cups cooked chicken
1/2 cup salsa
1 cup shredded cheddar cheese
2 green onions chopped (more for garnish)
1 tsp cumin
1 tsp garlic powder
1 tsp onion salt
1/2 tsp black pepper
1/2 tsp oregano
Six 8-inch flour tortillas
2 TBL butter, melted
Cooking Spray

Directions

1. Preheat oven to 400°.
2. Mix chicken, salsa, cheese, green onions, and spices in bowl.
3. Divide mixture evenly among center of tortillas.
4. Fold opposite sides of tortillas over filling.
5. Fold both ends up then place seam side down on Pam sprayed baking sheet.
6. Brush with melted butter.
7. Bake until golden brown about 25 minutes.
8. Garnish with salsa, onions, cheese, and sour cream.
9. Serve with salsa on the side.

Chicken Pot Pie in Phyllo Dough

I love chicken pot pie, but have never been able to make it at home. This recipe is little labor intensive , but a fun twist on a traditional pot pie.

SERVES [2]

INGREDIENTS

8 TBL (1 stick) butter; divided
1 medium onion; finely chopped
2 celery sticks; sliced thin
1/4 cup shredded carrot
2 TBL flour
1 cup chicken broth
2 cups cooked, chopped chicken
1 tsp salt
1/4 tsp nutmeg
2 TBL parsley
2 eggs, beaten
12 phyllo sheets

DIRECTIONS

1. In a large skillet melt 4 TBL butter over medium heat
2. Add celery, onion, and carrot and cook until onion is tender; approximately 2 minutes.
4. Stir in flour and cook 1 minute without browning.
5. Gradually whisk in broth.
6. Stir constantly. until mixture is thickened and smooth.
7. Add chicken, salt, nutmeg, and parsley; stir.
8. Remove from heat and let cool for 10 minutes.
9. Preheat oven to 350°.
10. Melt remaining butter.
11. Stack 6 phyllo sheets per packet, brushing each sheet with butter as stacked.
12. Place half chicken mixture on each stack.
13. Make packet by folding ends in.
14. Place on lightly buttered cooking sheet; seam sides down.
15. Cook 30 minutes until golden brown.
16. Serve.

Kelly's Shrimp and Crab Enchiladas

I loved ChiChi's® shrimp and crab enchiladas but could never find a recipe to duplicate it until Kelly shared hers with me. It is somewhat labor intensive, but so good it's worth the effort.

SERVES [2]

INGREDIENTS

Filling
1 TBL olive oil
1-1/2 cups raw shrimp; medium size cut in half
2 cloves garlic; minced
16 oz real crab meat
1 tsp dried parsley

Sauce
6 TBL butter
1/2 cup flour
3 1/2 cups milk
1 cup sour cream
2 cups Mexican style shredded cheese; divided
8 medium-sized flour tortilla

DIRECTIONS

1. Preheat the oven to 400°.
2. Drizzle the olive oil into the pan and add shrimp and garlic.
3. Saute for 2 minutes then add crab and parsley.
4. Season with salt and pepper.
5. Saute for 3 more minutes and remove from heat.
6. Remove from heat and stir in 1/2 cup of the cheese.
7. In a medium size saucepan, melt butter over medium heat.
8. Once butter is melted, add the flour to create a roux; stir constantly for one minute.
9. Add milk and sour cream. Whisk the mixture together and heat for 2-3 minutes until it starts to thicken.
10. Add 1 cup of the sauce to the shrimp and crab mixture and stir.
11. Add 1/2 cup sauce to the bottom of a large baking dish.
12. Place shrimp and crab mixture across each tortilla and roll up.
13. Place seam side down in the baking dish.
14. Pour remaining sauce over the top of the enchiladas, spread to cover if needed, then sprinkle the remaining 1 cup cheese over the top.
15. Sprinkled with a little paprika for color
16. Bake for 15-20 minutes until sauce is bubbly and cheese is melted.
17. Serve with green onions sprinkled on top

Chinese Seafood Nest

This recipe is a ton of work and has lots of ingredients, but ended up being very close to my favorite Chinese restaurant entree.

SERVES [2]

INGREDIENTS

1 pound Chinese egg noodles
1 TBL sesame oil
2 TBL fish sauce
2 TBL soy sauce
2 TBL oyster sauce
2 TBL corn starch
2 TBL sugar
2 TBL vegetable oil
2 Cloves garlic, minced
1 small yellow onion, sliced
3 oz Imitation or real Crab Meat
4 oz Shrimp,
3 oz Broccoli flowers
3 oz snow pea pods
1 small can mushrooms
4 Stalks green onion;chopped

DIRECTIONS

1. Mix fish sauce, soy sauce, oyster sauce, cornstarch, and sugar.
2. Bring water to boil in a large pot and place loosened noodles in boiling water; cover with water.
3. Boil noodles for 5 minutes; rinse in a colander and drain well; mix sesame seed oil into noodles.
4. Place 3 TBL vegetable oil in a small skillet and heat to bubbling. Add half of the noodles covering the full bottom of the pan in an even layer.
5. Let noodles brown for approximately 5 minutes on medium heat.
6. Flip noodle nest over and cook another 5 minutes.
7. Repeat steps for a second noodle nest.
8. Heat wok or large skillet with 2 TBL vegetable oil.
9. Add garlic and yellow onion; cook 2-3 minutes until garlic is slightly brown and onion is translucent.
10. Add shrimp; stir continuously until shrimp turns bright pink.
11. Add broccoli, mushrooms, and crab meat. Stir until broccoli is slightly tender.
12. Add snow peas stir until warm.
13. Add sauce and green onions; stir well.
14. Serve seafood mix over noodle nests on plate.

Desserts

··

I rarely cooked deserts when the kids were growing up, but hanging out with fellow RVers has shown me that a little something sweet at the end of a meal can be pretty special. Unfortunately buying deserts in the store is expensive and usually the quality is not nearly as good as what you can make at home. That being said, I think baking is one of the most challenging types of cooking in an RV. To help with that, most of these recipes are simple and allow some leeway on ingredients and bake times. If you are a meticulous baker, I definitely recommend investing in a good convection oven. Since we don't have one, these recipes are all just fine prepared with our standard RV propane oven.

Deb's Olive Oil Ice Cream

Deb made this one night and I was extremely dubious. Olive oil and ice cream? Oh my, was I wrong. If you haven't had this you have to give it a try.

SERVES [1]

INGREDIENTS

Vanilla Ice Cream; (Tillamook® is my favorite
High quality virgin olive oil
Sea salt

DIRECTIONS

1. Scoop a generous portion of ice cream.
2. Drizzle high quality olive oil on top.
3. Add a couple of pinches of sea salt.
4. Serve.

Aunt Cathy's Quick and Easy Turtles

When my Aunt Cathy read the blog and saw what we were trying to do, she definitely got into the spirit of it and sent a recipe for these quick and easy turtles. Simple, easy to make, and relatively inexpensive they are the perfect desert for the wandering lifestyle.

SERVES [12]

INGREDIENTS

1 bag Rolo candies
1 bag Snyder's of Hanover square shaped butter pretzels
Small bag pecan halves or peanut halves

DIRECTIONS

1. Preheat oven to 375°.
2. Unwrap Rolo® Candies.
3. Line baking sheet with wax paper.
4. Set one Rolo® on each pretzel.
5. Place in oven for approximately 5 minutes to soften candy. Do not allow them to melt.
6. Take out of oven and push a pecan half or two peanut halves into softened chocolate. *They are also good without nuts for those with allergies..*
7. Allow to cool and serve.
8. Store leftovers in a Ziploc® baggie.

Poke Cake

This desert is propane oven friendly, simple, and delicious.

SERVES [8]

INGREDIENTS

1 completely baked and cooled square cake layer
1 cups boiling water
Two 3 oz gelatin packages; any flavor
Whipped Topping

DIRECTIONS

1. Pierce cake layers with fork every 1/2-inch.
2. Completely dissolve <u>gelatin powder</u> with 1 cup boiling water.
3. Stir for 2 minutes.
4. Carefully pour gelatin over cake layer.
5. Refrigerate for 3 hours.
6. Dip cake pan in warm water 10 seconds; invert cake onto a serving plate.
7. Spread with 1 cup of whipped topping.

Tracy's Quick Applesauce Cake

I spent a summer in Alaska work kamping and made deserts every Monday, Wednesday, and Friday night. By far the most popular desert was my applesauce cake. You can substitute no sugar cake mix and applesauce and it still tastes great as a low sugar option

SERVES [8]

INGREDIENTS

¼ cup sugar or sugar substitute
2 tsp ground cinnamon
½ cup butter or margarine, softened
One 16 oz can applesauce (no sugar added)
 3 eggs
One 18 oz package of yellow cake

DIRECTIONS

1. Blend sugar and cinnamon.
2. Grease cake pan and dust with 1 TBL sugar/cinnamon mixture.
3. Blend margarine, eggs, applesauce, and cake mix.
4. Reserve 1 ½ cups batter.
5. Pour remaining batter into pan.
6. Sprinkle with remaining sugar/cinnamon mixture then top with reserved batter.
7. Bake at 350° for 35-45 minutes .
8. Cool cake in pan for 15 minutes then invert on serving tray.

Sugar Free Oatmeal Raisin Cookies

Don't tell people these are sugar free and they will seriously have no idea.

SERVES [6]

INGREDIENTS

1-1/2 cups all-purpose flour
1 tsp baking soda
1 tsp ground cinnamon
1 cup butter, softened
1 cup sugar substitute
2 large eggs
1 tablespoon molasses
1-1/2 tsp vanilla extract
3 cups old-fashioned oatmeal, uncooked
1 cup raisins

DIRECTIONS

1. Preheat oven to 350°.
2. Stir together flour, soda, and cinnamon. Set aside.
3. Beat butter and Splenda® at medium speed with an electric mixer until fluffy. Add eggs, molasses and vanilla, beating until blended. Gradually add flour mixture, beating at low speed until blended.
4. Stir in oats and raisins.
5. Drop dough by rounded tablespoons onto lightly greased baking sheets.
6. Bake 10 to 12 minutes or until lightly browned. Cool slightly on baking sheets. Remove to wire racks; cool completely.

Sugar Free Apple Crescents

Love the taste of apple pie, but don't want to mess with making one?
These easy apple crescents get you close with much less work.

Serves [4]

Ingredients

1 pkg refrigerated crescent rolls
1/8 cup sugar substitute
1/2 TBL cinnamon
2 medium tart apples; peeled, cored, and quartered
2 TBL margarine or butter; melted
Cooking Spray
1/8 cup walnuts; optional
1/8 cup raisins; optional

Directions

1. Preheat oven to 375°.
2. Spray a cooking sheet with butter flavored cooking spray.
3. Combine cinnamon and sugar; mix well.
4. Unroll crescent dough and separate into 8 triangles
5. Sprinkle triangles with cinnamon/sugar mixture; leave some for tops.
6. Place an apple quarter near the short, triangle side and roll-up.
7. Place on baking sheet; seam side down.
8. If desired press walnuts and/or raisins into dough.
9. Drizzle with melted butter.
10. Sprinkle remaining cinnamon-sugar mix on top.
11. Bake for 20-25 minutes until golden brown on top.
12. Serve warm. *Delicious right out of the oven but do not heat up well.*

Rhubarb and Apple Crisp

Rhubarb is pretty popular in the northern states, but I was always intimidated by it as an ingredient In Alaska, rhubarb was plentiful, so I tried several recipes and this one was by far my favorite.

SERVES [8]

INGREDIENTS

3/4 cup sugar
3 TBL cornstarch
3 cups 2" sliced fresh rhubarb
2 cups bite sized apples, strawberries, or blueberries
1 cup old-fashioned oats
1/2 cup brown sugar; packed
1/2 cup real butter,;melted
1/3 cup all purpose flour
1 tsp cinnamon

DIRECTIONS

1. In a large bowl combine sugar and cornstarch; mix well.
2. Add chopped rhubarb and apples; toss to coat.
3. Spoon into an 8 " square baking dish.
4. In a separate small bowl combine oats, brown sugar, flour, and cinnamon; mix well.
5. Add melted butter and mix until resembles coarse crumbs.
6. Sprinkle crumbs over fruit.
7. Bake at 350° for 45 minutes or until bubbly and fruit is tender.
8. Let sit for 15 minutes.
9. Serve warm preferably with half a scoop of vanilla ice cream.

Pina Colada Cake

I had to have at least one recipe with alcohol in it so I chose one that taste a little like a Pina Colada. Spiced Rum makes this really good along with its sinful frosting

SERVES [8]

INGREDIENTS

Cake Ingredients
1 box yellow cake mix
1 pkg instant vanilla pudding
4 eggs
3/4 cup coconut water
1/4 cup oil
1/3 cup spiced rum

Frosting
One 8 oz container
Cool Whip
1 small can
 crushed pineapple
1 pkg instant vanilla pudding
2 TBL spiced rum
1 cup flaked coconut
(optional)

DIRECTIONS

1. Preheat oven to 350°.
2. Grease a 13x9 cake pan.
3. Mix cake ingredients and beat with an electric mixer for at least 2 minutes.
4. Spread batter evenly in pan.
5. Cook for 20-25 minutes until butter knife goes into center of cake and comes out clean.
6. Allow cake to cool.
7. Mix frosting ingredients well and frost cake.
8. Optionally sprinkle top of frosting with 1 cup coconut flakes.

Lee's Apple Pie

Lee's favorite dessert is dutch apple pie, or apple pie with a crumb topping. After trying store bought pies across the country, I finally decided to try and make one myself. It turned out pretty well.

SERVES [6]

INGREDIENTS

Pillsbury refrigerated pie dough
6 medium-size tart apples; peeled, cored, and sliced
1 cup sugar
2 cups of graham cracker crumbs; crushed fine
1/2 cup all purpose flour
1/2 tsp cinnamon
1/2 cup butter or margarine; melted

DIRECTIONS

1. Preheat oven to 350°.
2. Place pastry in pie shell and crimp edges with back side of fork.
3. Combine sugar, flour, and cinnamon.
4. Sprinkle over apples.
5. Sprinkle graham cracker crumbs evenly over top.
6. Pour butter evenly over topping.
7. Place foil around edges of pie.
8. Cook about 1 hour until crumble top is browned.
9. Let cool and serve at room temperature or chilled.

Grandma Murray's Carrot Cake

I love well made carrot cake, but have never had one as good as Bill's. He generously shared the recipe but said credit had to go to his Grandma Murray.

INGREDIENTS

Dry:
2 cups flour
2 tsp baking powder
1-1/2 tsp baking soda
1 tsp salt
2 tsp cinnamon
1 tsp nutmeg
1 tsp ground cloves

Wet:
2 cups sugar
1-1/2 cups vegetable oil
4 large eggs

Extras (add last):
2 Cups grated carrots (4-6 larger size carrots)
One 16 oz can very well drained crushed pineapple
Well chopped maraschino cherries (well drained 10 oz glass jar)

Optional:
3/4 cup chopped nuts (walnuts or pecans)
1/2 cup shredded coconut 1/2 cup raisins

Cream Cheese Frosting
8 oz cream cheese (room temp)
1 stick real butter (room temp)
6 TBL powder (confectionery) sugar
2 tsp vanilla extract

DIRECTIONS

1. Sift together 7 dry ingredients - set aside.
2. Mix 3 wet ingredients in mixer.
3. Add dry ingredients and mix well.
4. Add extra ingredients and mix well.
5. Place half of the batter in cake pan and bake at 350° until butter knife can be placed in center and come out clean. (13x9 took roughly fifty-five minutes) (8x8 took roughly forty minutes).
6. Use extra batter for a second cake.

Homemade Cream Cheese Frosting
1. Mix cream cheese and butter together.
2. Add sugar and vanilla and blend on medium high until well blended.
3. Frost after cake is completely cold.

Thank you and I hope you enjoyed this book. You can read more about our full timing lifestyle at www.camperchronicles.com.

Tracy Perkins

Copyright © 2017 by Tracy S. Perkins
All rights reserved. This book or any portion thereof
may not be reproduced or used in any manner whatsoever without the express written permission of the author.

www.camperchronicles.com

Made in the USA
San Bernardino, CA
04 December 2017